Date: 10/6/14

WILD HORSES

LIVING WILD

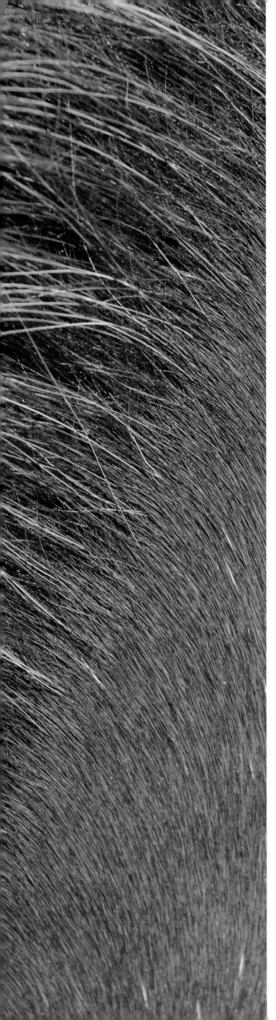

LIVING WILD

Published by Creative Education
P.O. Box 227, Mankato, Minnesota 56002
Creative Education is an imprint of The Creative Company
www.thecreativecompany.us

Design and production by Mary Herrmann
Art direction by Rita Marshall
Printed in the United States of America

Photographs by Alamy (AF archive, Images & Stories, Nancy G Western Photography/Nancy Greifenhagen), Dreamstime (Arvacsaba, Asimagery, GaryAlvis, Maria Itina, Gea Strucks), iStockphoto (cassp, Dennis Donohue, dortega, igorzynik, karenparker2000, Lucasdm, Julie Marshall, photonaj, zorandimzr), Shutterstock (Anton Balazh, Nicole Ciscato, jo Crebbin, Dennis Donohue, Wendy Farrington, Horse Crazy, Im Perfect Lazybones, justasc, Kamzara, Lenkadan, mariait, J. Marijs, KACHALKIN OLEG, outdoorsman, Maxim Petrichuk, Anastasija Popova, Tanya Puntti, Galushko Sergey, Makarova Viktoria, Steve Wilson), SuperStock (Album/Florilegius/Album), Wikipedia (Tony Hisgett, David Starner)

Library of Congress Cataloging-in-Publication Data
Gish, Melissa.
Wild horses / Melissa Gish.
p. cm. — (Living wild)
Includes bibliographical references and index.
Summary: A scientific look at wild horses, including their habitats, physical characteristics such as their manes, behaviors, relationships with humans, and numbers of the swift equids in the world today.
ISBN 978-1-60818-420-0
1. Wild horses—Juvenile literature. 2. Horses—Juvenile literature. I. Title. II. Series: Living wild.

SF360.G57 2014
599.665'5—dc23   2013031815

CCSS: RI.5.1, 2, 3, 8; RST.6-8.1, 2, 5, 6, 8; RH.6-8.3, 4, 5, 6, 7, 8

First Edition
9 8 7 6 5 4 3 2 1

CREATIVE EDUCATION

WILD HORSES

Melissa Gish

In Custer National Forest, the early May sunshine fills a cloudless sky. A wild horse stands with her powerful front legs braced for a climb up the foothills.

In Custer National Forest, the early May sunshine fills a cloudless sky, melting the last snow on the Pryor Mountains while nourishing patches of spring grass. A wild horse stands with her powerful front legs braced for a climb up the foothills. She raises her head, nostrils flaring, and sniffs the air. She opens her mouth, takes a deep breath, and lets out a loud whinny. A half dozen other horses gather around her.

She swings her head, nudging them and snorting. Then she bolts up the mossy slope toward a stream lined with tall grass. A mature male horse follows the group, eyes and ears alert. The horses feast on the tender grass and drink from the stream. One of the females slips away from the group. She finds a secluded spot in a stand of limber pines— the perfect place to give birth to the first horse of the new spring.

WHERE IN THE WORLD THEY LIVE

■ **North American Mustang**
American West, Atlantic islands

■ **Brumby**
Australia

■ **Przewalski's Horse**
Mongolia

Most of the "wild" horses in the world today could better be described as "feral," since they returned to a wild state after having been domesticated. North America's mustangs and Australia's brumbies are the most well known of this group. However, Mongolia's Przewalski's horses were never domesticated, and this rare subspecies is the last of Earth's truly wild horses. The colored squares represent common locations of all three horses.

RUNNING WILD

T he seven living members of the genus *Equus* (*EE-kwis*), which means "horse" in Latin, include three species of wild ass, three species of zebra, and the horse. Members of this genus are called equids. About 54 million years ago, the first horses, 11-inch-tall (28 cm) "dawn horses," lived in North America. Over millions of years, they **evolved** into many different kinds of horses. When the first humans to travel from Asia to North America crossed the Bering **Land Bridge** about 12,000 years ago, horses became an important food source. The North American horses retreated to other parts of the world, and those that remained on the continent soon became **extinct**.

Horses did not return to North America until Spanish explorers reintroduced them in the early 1500s. All North American wild horses, called mustangs, are descendants of **domesticated** Spanish horses that escaped captivity centuries ago. The word "mustang" is derived from the Spanish *mesteño*, which refers to an ownerless or stray horse. Most of North America's mustangs—numbering more than 20,000—live in Nevada, but they can be found roaming

More than 2.3 million mustangs existed in 1900, but hunting for horsemeat slashed the population to about 10,000 by 1970.

Semi-feral Polish Koniks were used by German and Russian troops to carry supplies during World War I.

grasslands in nine other western states from Montana to New Mexico. Some wild horses also live on islands off the Atlantic coast of Maryland, Virginia, and North Carolina.

Like the mustangs of the American West, Australia's brumbies are the **feral** descendants of horses that escaped or were released when the first Europeans visited Australia in the late 1700s. The word "brumby" likely comes from the **Aboriginal** word *baroomby*, meaning "wild." The Przewalski's (*sheh-VAWL-skees*) horse is native to Mongolia and is considered the last truly wild horse on the planet because it was never domesticated.

Horses are mammals. All mammals produce milk to feed their young and, with the exceptions of the egg-laying platypuses and echidnas of Australia, give birth to live offspring. Mammals are also warm-blooded. This means that their bodies try to maintain a healthy, constant temperature that is usually warmer than their surroundings. To stay warm, horses grow shaggy coats of winter hair, and in summer, they sweat—just like humans. The sweat **evaporates** to cool the blood just beneath the skin.

Horses are characterized by their straight cutting teeth, long necks and heads, and powerful legs. Each leg has a

Because brumbies are descended from a variety of European and Arabian horses, they are hardy animals.

Przewalski's (shown) and other horses we know today split from a common ancestor about 160,000 years ago.

single toe covered by a tough hoof. The bottom of the hoof is spongy and works like a shock absorber. The top of the hoof is thick and hard. Because wild horses spend their time on open ranges, their hooves are thicker and more durable than those of domestic horses. Hooves grow continuously, and while domestic horses must have their hooves trimmed, the hooves of wild horses are naturally worn down from constant use on rocky terrain.

Przewalski's horses are dull gold (a color called dun) or tan in color with pale gold or white on the belly and around the **muzzle**. A dark brown stripe runs down the center of the back, and dark markings cover the lower legs, which are called fetlocks. Przewalski's horses also have a stiff length of hair, called a mane, running down the back of the neck. Mustangs have longer, flowing manes as well as a forelock—a long patch of hair that grows from between the ears and drapes down over the forehead. Mustangs vary in color from black to various shades of gray or brown to dun, blond, and white. Many mustangs have markings on their fetlocks and faces, but some have spots on their bodies as well. Depending on the type of pattern, spotted horses can be classified as dappled,

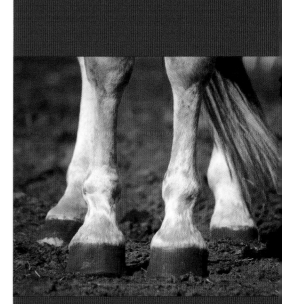

Horses can suffer a variety of hoof ailments, from viral diseases to cracking because of overexposure to water.

Connected to nerves under the skin, a horse's highly sensitive muzzle whiskers are useful in investigating by touch.

pinto (or paint), or Appaloosa. The muzzle is covered with short, velvety fur and scattered whiskers.

Wild horses generally weigh from 500 to 800 pounds (227–363 kg). They stand about 4.5 feet (1.4 m) at the shoulder and stretch just less than 7 feet (2.1 m) from the tip of the nose to the rump. Mustang males (called stallions) can grow somewhat larger, standing 5 feet (1.5 m) at the shoulder and weighing up to 1,000 pounds (454 kg). Despite their size, adult wild horses eat only five to six pounds (2.3–2.7 kg) of food a day. As herbivores, they eat only vegetation. Most of a wild horse's diet is grass, but shrubs, berries, and twigs provide food as well. Horses cannot vomit, which makes them susceptible to illness if they eat spoiled or moldy vegetation or drink polluted water. Wild horses need water every day. They gather at lakesides, springs, streams, rivers, and even watering ponds created for domestic cattle and sheep.

A horse's front teeth, called incisors, are designed for clipping grass close to the ground. The back teeth, called molars, are sharply ridged for grinding food into a pulp. Horses have four pairs of molars in each jaw. A horse's teeth keep growing throughout its life, but constant

chewing prevents the molars from becoming too long. Horses can "hear" through their teeth. As they graze, horses feel vibrations in the ground that travel along the jawbone to the **auditory** system, alerting them to the approach of other horses—or predators.

Wild horses also hear sounds that travel through the

Naturally free-roaming, mustangs are constantly on the move, searching for food and evading predators.

Horses born with white facial markings retain those markings—completely unchanged—their entire lives.

air. They can pivot their ears to detect sounds from all directions. And with their eyes set wide apart and high on their heads, horses can see almost all the way around themselves without turning their heads. Because of their long muzzle, horses have a blind spot of four to five feet (1.2–1.5 m) directly in front of their faces, so they typically bob their heads when looking around. At the slightest indication of danger, horses will run.

A wild horse is able to change directions and speed quickly. The typical running speed, called a gallop, is 25 to 30 miles (40.2–48.3 km) per hour, but wild horses are able to run up to 40 miles (64 km) per hour in short bursts. They also have a highly acute sense of smell that enables them to detect scents from more than a mile (1.6 km) away. They do this using a special area on the roof of the mouth called the Jacobson's organ. When a horse catches a whiff of something interesting, it will open its mouth and curl its upper lip to inhale the air. This gesture makes the horse appear to be laughing, but it is actually focusing on the chemical signals in the air that help it recognize and locate the source of the odor, be it another horse, a predator, or food.

North American mustangs were captured and broken by 17th- and 18th-century Spanish cowboys called vaqueros.

Ancestors of today's wild mustangs were first domesticated 6,000 years ago in what is now the Republic of Kazakhstan.

Stallions may fight over leadership, but they do not fight to the death—the weaker horse simply gives up.

NOMADS OF THE PRAIRIE

orses go by different names throughout the stages of their lives. Foals are baby horses less than one year old. At one year old, they are yearlings. After this, young females are called fillies, while males are called colts. A young female remains a filly until age four or until she breeds, at which time she becomes a mare. When colts mature, between the ages of four and seven, they become bachelors. Horses live in family groups called bands, which contain anywhere from 3 to 15 individuals. These highly structured social groups, led by a dominant mare and stallion, typically contain a number of other mares and their offspring.

Most often, bachelors are driven from the band by stallions and roam together in bachelor bands. When a bachelor grows old enough—and strong enough—to establish his own band, he may first create a harem of fillies by stealing the fillies from rival bands. By breeding with his new group members, the young male becomes a stallion and forms a new band. A bachelor may also challenge another stallion to a fight to take over leadership of an existing band.

Bands are semi-nomadic, meaning they travel around

In the western states, pronghorn (above) and mule deer often graze near bands of wild horses, counting on the stallions to alert them of danger.

The horses on Assateague Island have survived numerous natural disasters such as hurricanes and floods over the years.

in a selected area called a home range, grazing until resources in one spot are nearly depleted and then moving to another spot. Home ranges may be several square miles or several thousand square miles in size, depending on the availability of food and water resources. As a band travels, the dominant mare is usually found at the front, leading the members to food and water. The stallion usually travels behind the others, protecting the band members from predators and defending his leadership position from intruding males that try to steal his mares or take over his band. He will allow his daughters to be stolen, but he will fight fiercely to protect his mares. While the band grazes, the stallion remains watchful.

Wild horses can live well into their 30s. Females are ready to mate when they are about four years old, and stallions begin to mate at age six or seven. The leader of a band will mate with all the mares in his band but not with his own female offspring. A stallion's daughters are allowed to breed with other males in the band or with stallions that steal the fillies for their own bands. It is not uncommon for a filly to be stolen several times before she mates and gives birth. She will then usually remain with the father of her foal and continue to mate with him for her entire life.

The mating season lasts from April to July in North America and Europe and from March to June in Australia. The **gestation** period for horses is 11 months. When the

Scientists once believed that Koniks were a surviving form of a Eurasian wild horse known as the Tarpan.

time comes for a mare to give birth, she leaves the band and finds a secluded spot. She gives birth to a single foal while lying on her side. Twins are rare. At birth, wild foals weigh about 5 percent of their mother's weight, which means that an 800-pound (363 kg) mare would give birth to a foal weighing about 40 pounds (18.1 kg). Foals are born with their eyes open. They can stand up within an hour of birth, and they also drink their mother's milk for the first time.

During the first 12 to 24 hours after giving birth, mares produce special milk called colostrum. This milk is rich with **nutrients** and antibodies that protect the foal from disease and infection. Foals typically nurse once or twice every hour for several minutes. They can drink 3 to 4 gallons (11.4–15.1 l) of milk in a 24-hour period. A healthy, excited foal is able to run within two hours of birth. It quickly tires, however, and after taking a few laps around its mother, a foal will typically lie back down for a nap. For the first few days of its life, the foal is kept away from the other members of its band because it must learn to recognize its mother's voice and scent. This behavior is called imprinting, and it will enable the foal to always find its mother—especially in the flurry of a stampede to evade predators. After about three days, the mare and foal rejoin the band. Licking and rubbing are important communication behaviors among members of a band, and even normally aloof stallions may groom their offspring.

Although foals begin eating grass within two weeks, they rely on their mother's milk for nourishment for the first five to seven months of their lives. By this time, roughly 70 percent of their nutrition will come from vegetation. Despite its grazing habits, a closely bonded foal may nurse from its mother for more than a year or until its mother gives birth to another foal. At about three

Whether they are wild, feral, or domesticated, all mares will fiercely defend their foals against perceived dangers.

Horses can taste even slight differences in water flavor and often select favorite water sources to frequent.

months of age, foals begin playing with each other. Play-fighting helps males learn survival and dominance skills in preparation for forming and defending their own bands, while behaviors such as chasing, nudging, and nipping help all foals develop their communication and social **hierarchy** skills. Young horses remain with their mothers until the males leave to join other bands or the females are stolen and forced into neighboring harems.

Healthy adult horses have few natural enemies, but young, old, and sick horses may fall prey to cougars, bears, and wolf packs. Even bobcats and coyotes may prey on foals. The main predator of Przewalski's horses is the wolf. When faced with a threat, a band of wild horses will try to protect foals by wrangling them into the center of the band as they run. Because horses have been prey animals since the days of the dawn horse, their first instinct when faced with danger is always to run—never to fight. Only when cornered with nowhere to run will a stallion kick and bite to defend his band. Historically, the greatest threat to wild horses has been humans. For centuries, shrinking habitats, capture, and slaughter have had major effects on wild horse populations.

Dartmoor ponies, which are 45 to 50 inches (114–127 cm) tall, are semi-feral horses protected in southwestern England.

As part of his mural The History of Mexico, Mexican artist Diego Rivera showed Cortés's arrival in the New World.

N o other animal reflects the spirit of freedom that represents the American West like the wild mustang. The story of wild mustangs in North America began on March 4, 1519, when Spanish conquistador Hernán Cortés landed his ships in Mexico with 508 men and 16 horses aboard. Cortés was looking for gold and wanted to conquer the Aztec people of Mexico and take over their city, Tenochtitlán (now Mexico City). However, the Aztec emperor, Montezuma, refused to surrender to Cortés.

The Aztecs had never seen cannons or horses before. When Cortés fired his cannons and brought his men on horseback before Montezuma's men, they were terrified, calling the horses and riders "beasts with two heads and six legs." More conquistadors landed in Mexico with more men on horseback. The Aztecs fought to defend their city, but they were no match for the Spaniards' mounted army. By 1521, the Aztecs were defeated, and Cortés wrote to Queen Isabella of Spain, "We owe it all to God and the horse."

As more Europeans sailed to North America, more horses arrived with them. Horses that escaped or were

Painted horses are still a common sight at American Indian tribal powwows, or special gatherings.

Warring American Indians often painted symbols on their horses with natural substances such as clay, blood, egg yolks, or berries.

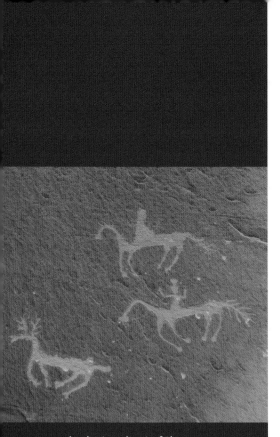

Ancient rock art of the Anasazi people is preserved at Canyon de Chelly National Monument in Arizona.

turned loose went feral and multiplied, forming massive herds of wild horses that ranged across half the continent, from the Mississippi River to the Pacific Ocean. American Indians learned to tame and ride the wild horses, leading to major changes in the **cultures** of many tribes, most notably the tribes of the Great Plains. Horses allowed people to move more easily and quickly from place to place, which increased trade, hunting capabilities, and warfare. By the late 18th century, the Plains Indians had become what historians call a horse culture, capturing wild horses to hunt the plentiful bison that roamed the sprawling prairies and bountiful foothills that stretched from Mexico into Canada.

The Przewalski's horse formed the basis of the Mongolians' horse culture long before the Plains Indians adopted a nomadic lifestyle. Horses allowed the Huns, under several rulers (including Attila from A.D. 434 to 453), to build an empire that spanned from China to Germany and lasted for 100 years. However, unlike the horses of North America, which could be tamed, the Przewalski's horses remained wild, even when captured and ridden. Because these horses could not be domesticated, they never became work animals and were kept only as food. In fact,

they became **nuisance** animals to Asian farmers. Stallions stole mares that farmers had corralled for meat, and bands broke down fences to graze on crops.

The Przewalski's horse shared the land with prehistoric humans, as evidenced by artwork featuring these horses from what is now France. The image of a horse's head etched into the rock of Combarelles Cave dates to 13,000 years ago, and horses painted on a cave wall in Lascaux date back 17,000 years. Horses also appear in Grotto Chauvet, where the world's oldest cave art—dating back 30,000 years—has been found. Cave and rock art depicting wild mustangs, though much more abundant, is much younger. Hundreds of examples of petroglyphs, or

Przewalski's horses have a uniform look, unlike modern domestic horses, which have been crossed with many breeds.

BRUMBY'S RUN

It lies beyond the Western Pines
Towards the sinking sun,
And not a survey mark defines
The bounds of "Brumby's Run."

On odds and ends of mountain land,
On tracks of range and rock
Where no one else can make a stand,
Old Brumby rears his stock.

A wild, unhandled lot they are
Of every shape and breed.
They venture out 'neath moon and star
Along the flats to feed;

But when the dawn makes pink the sky
And steals along the plain,
The Brumby horses turn and fly
Towards the hills again.

The traveller by the mountain-track
May hear their hoof-beats pass,
And catch a glimpse of brown and black
Dim shadows on the grass.

The eager stockhorse pricks his ears
And lifts his head on high
In wild excitement when he hears
The Brumby mob go by.

Old Brumby asks no price or fee
O'er all his wide domains:
The man who yards his stock is free
To keep them for his pains.

So, off to scour the mountain-side
With eager eyes aglow,
To strongholds where the wild mobs hide
The gully-rakers go.

A rush of horses through the trees,
A red shirt making play;
A sound of stockwhips on the breeze,
They vanish far away!

Ah, me! before our day is done
We long with bitter pain
To ride once more on Brumby's Run
And yard his mob again.

by Andrew Barton Paterson (1864–1941)

images engraved into rock faces, exist throughout North America. The Tolar Petroglyph Site in Wyoming includes images of horses painted on limestone outcroppings along Bitter Creek. The artwork was made by early 18th-century Comanche Indians, who regularly traveled to Mexico and what is now the state of New Mexico to bring horses back to Wyoming. Comanche rock art discovered in 2004 in Farrington Springs, Colorado, depicts armored horses with riders—images of Spanish soldiers—and dates to between the years 1700 and 1750.

Thundering herds of wild horses in the American West still bring to mind an image of pride and strength that people admire. It's no wonder that numerous sports teams adopted the mustang as their symbol. Musty the Mustang is the mascot of California Polytechnic State University, and Gunrock the Mustang represents the University of California, Davis. Mustang stallions are also called mavericks, which is the name adopted by sports teams at the University of Texas at Arlington. Each year, a university student is selected to wear a costume to play Blaze, a white stallion with a blue mane. White and blue are also the colors used in the National Basketball Association's Dallas

A horse's body temperature normally drops from 101 °F (38.3 °C) in summer to 97 °F (36.1 °C) in winter.

British Columbia's Elegesi Qayus Wild Horse Preserve contains as many as 1,000 wild horses managed by the Tsilhqot'in First Nations tribe.

Nations such as the Philippines and Haiti used the P-51 Mustang well into the 1970s.

Before horses, American Indians used dogs to carry packs, so horses were often called elk dogs, spirit dogs, or simply big dogs.

Mavericks logo, which features the head of a wild stallion.

The P-51 Mustang was a fighter airplane introduced during World War II. Its speed and maneuverability in the air reflected its namesake's power and agility across the prairies of the American West. During America's involvement in the war (1941–45), America's fleet of P-51 Mustangs shot down nearly 5,000 enemy aircraft. The success of the P-51 Mustang inspired designers at Ford Motor Company to name their latest sports car, introduced in 1964, the Mustang. One of the best-known American automobiles in history, the Mustang has remained in production to this day and was responsible for launching a new style of automobile. Called pony cars, automobiles such as the Mustang were designed with long hoods and short rear decks—and, like the spirits of America's wild horses, with big, powerful engines. From 1969 to 1977, the Mustang had a companion in the Ford Maverick. With a body style similar to the Mustang's (featuring a long hood and continuously sloping roofline), the Maverick became nearly as popular as its big brother.

Real mustangs and mavericks have been a staple of Western movies since the early days of Hollywood. The

1926 silent movie *The Devil Horse*, featuring Rex, King of the Wild Horses, was one of the first to feature a horse in a leading role. Legendary horseman and performer Frank Hopkins was a supporter of using wild mustangs as performers in the 1890s and early 1900s, and he later wrote about the wild mustangs he captured and rode. Hopkins boasted that he and the mustang, named Hidalgo, once won a 3,000-mile (4,828 km) race across the Arabian Peninsula—a feat that served as the basis for the 2004 movie *Hidalgo*. Hopkins also worked to protect wild horses from abuse and slaughter.

The artist who created the fictional horse named Spirit for the animated 2002 DreamWorks Animation movie *Spirit: Stallion of the Cimarron* based Spirit on a real-life mustang named Donner, who was captured in Oregon and relocated to the Return to Freedom American Wild Horse Sanctuary in California, where he celebrated his 18th birthday in 2013. A real-life stallion known as Cloud was the subject of a series of books and documentaries on the wild horses of the Pryor Mountains in southern Montana. Supporters of Cloud the Stallion and his band can like his Facebook page and follow his activities.

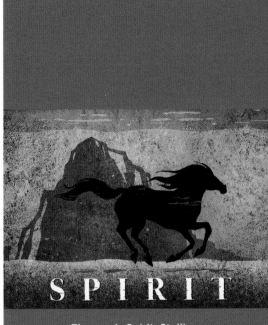

SPIRIT

The movie Spirit: Stallion of the Cimarron *used the sounds of real horses for any vocalizations.*

Horses were traditionally measured by a "hand," which has been standardized to mean four inches (10.2 cm) today.

Unlike the dawn horse, Mesohippus had six grinding teeth that allowed it to feed on grass.

A LEGACY OF FREEDOM

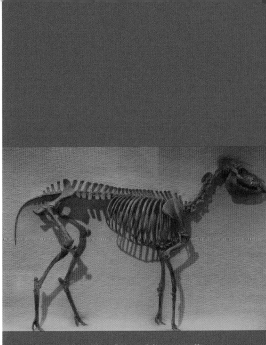

Fossils of Mesohippus *tell scientists this horse ancestor walked on the second of its three toes—the start of a hoof.*

T he earliest horse ancestors, the dawn horses, belonged to a group of small mammals in the genus *Eohippus* (or *Hyracotherium*), which existed in North America and Europe from 55 to 34 million years ago. These animals had four toes on each front leg and three toes on each back leg. Lacking grinding molars, they fed on berries and leaves. Twice as big as dawn horses, animals in the genus *Mesohippus*, or "middle horse," existed between 37 and 30 million years ago. They stood about two feet (0.6 m) tall at the shoulder and possessed teeth suitable for eating leaves. Twice as big as *Mesohippus*, animals in the genus *Merychippus* began to more closely resemble modern horses. Living from about 17 to 10 million years ago, they began losing all but their center toe, which would eventually become a single hoof in animals of the genus *Pliohippus*, which emerged about 12 million years ago. When *Pliohippus* died out about 6 million years ago, modern horses began to evolve.

Fossils of prehistoric horses have been found on every continent except Australia and Antarctica. The first horse fossil was only a tooth. It was discovered in a stone quarry in Paris, France, in the 1820s. Further digging revealed many

An ancient genetic change called leopard complex is responsible for the Appaloosa's spotted pattern.

Many names are used to describe horses' varying colors: roan, chestnut, palomino, bay, buckskin, silver dapple, pinto, and paint.

fossilized skeletal remains of early horses in Paris around the same time that the famous 19th-century naturalist Charles Darwin found horse fossils in South America. Hundreds of fossil beds containing the remains of prehistoric horses exist across North America. Hagerman Fossil Beds National Monument in Idaho is considered by **paleontologists** to be one of the most important sites for the study of prehistoric horses. The Ashfall Fossil Beds State Historical Park in Nebraska and the Page Museum at the Rancho La Brea Tar Pits in Los Angeles, California, are also well known around the world for their prehistoric horse fossils.

Wild horses in Asia nearly went the way of their extinct ancestors. The Przewalski's horse is named for Nikolai Przhevalsky, a Russian explorer and naturalist who, in 1878, became one of the first non-Mongolians to document the wild horses of Asia, which are called the *takhi* ("spirits") in their native Mongolia. For 5,000 years, the Przewalski's horse flourished from Kazakhstan to western China, but overhunting and habitat loss beginning in the 19th century led to its extinction in the wild. The last wild horse was captured in 1947. Just 14 captive horses in the Czech Republic and Germany were all that remained.

Careful **captive-breeding** by several European nations increased the Przewalski's population to 300 by the mid-1970s. In 1977, the Foundation for the Preservation and Protection of the Przewalski's Horse was founded with the goal of organizing and monitoring a horse exchange program among zoos around the world to avoid **inbreeding** and thus safely increase the total population of Przewalski's horses. In 1992, the foundation was able to release 16 captive-bred horses into the wild in Mongolia, where the government established Hustai National Park specifically for the horses' protection. As of 2010, the

France's Camargue horses have lived in semi-feral conditions for centuries but are also used in herding cattle.

world's population of Przewalski's horses was about 1,800 animals, with 250 of those being free-ranging in wildlife reserves in Mongolia, Kazakhstan, and northern China.

In North America, all wild horses east of the Mississippi River are protected by law. About 300 wild horses live on Assateague Island, located on the Atlantic Ocean off the coast of Virginia and Maryland. They are called Chincoteague ponies on the Virginia side of the island and Assateague horses (or ponies) on the Maryland side. North Carolina's Outer Banks are home to about 400 wild horses, called Banker horses, and about 350 Sable Island ponies live on Sable Island, off the coast of Nova Scotia. Because food is limited in their island habitats, the stallions are no heavier than 790 pounds (360 kg). Many people believe that the island horses are descended from Spanish horses that swam to safety from shipwrecks in the 16th century.

Mustangs of the American West have endured a long history of persecution that continues today. For more than 200 years, cattle ranchers have seen wild horses as competitors for grazing land. Ranchers pressured the United States government to control wild horse populations, so in 1971, the Wild Free-Roaming Horse and Burro Act was passed. It put the Bureau of Land Management (BLM) in charge of managing wild horses on the 264 million acres (107 million ha) of public lands where they have roamed for centuries. It became the BLM's responsibility to determine and maintain an **ecological** balance between wild horses and the land and water resources they use.

Too many horses, the BLM concluded, existed in the wild, so an adoption program was established. Horses were rounded up using helicopters and horsemen. The

Candleberry twigs, dune grasses, rose hips, and sugary persimmons provide a varied diet for Assateague horses.

Many Canadian wild horses are found on Nova Scotia's Sable Island, in British Columbia's Brittany Triangle, and Alberta's Siffleur Wilderness Area.

Like their mustang relatives, the first burros (small donkeys) arrived in North America in the 1500s and number about 6,825 today.

horses were put into confinement facilities where they awaited adoption by private citizens or conservation groups. Not all horses were adopted, however, and tens of thousands of wild horses spent years in pens. In 2004, the law was changed to allow the confinement facilities to release unadopted horses for sale. Annual roundups continue today, with some horses being adopted and most being sold. A small amount of horsemeat is sent to zoos to feed carnivorous animals, but most of the meat is exported to Europe and Japan, where people eat it. Horsemeat cannot be legally sold as food in America. Animal rights groups introduced the American Horse Slaughter Prevention Act, which would stop the slaughter of horses for human consumption, but the U.S. government had yet to approve the measure as of 2013.

Today, about 34,000 wild horses run free in the West, but the BLM has determined that enough resources exist to support only about 20,000. Some conservationists argue that 20,000 is insufficient to maintain strong **genetic** diversity and fear that America's wild mustangs are heading toward extinction. Dreamcatcher Wild Horse and Burro Sanctuary in California, Sky Mountain Wild Horse

Sanctuary in New Mexico, and the Black Hills Wild Horse Sanctuary in South Dakota are just a few of the many wild horse sanctuaries that exist to help protect horses that are captured and either await adoption or are found to be unadoptable. But sanctuaries typically overflow with needy horses. Issues with population and resource management must be addressed with a combination of facts and compassion if we are to keep the spirit of the West alive in North America's wild horses.

Social grooming is an important behavior for horses as they reinforce family bonds and build relationships.

ANIMAL TALE: THE ELK DOGS

Long ago, the only means of travel was by foot, and dogs were used to carry packs as tribes followed the herds of bison. At this time in the foothills of Montana, there lived an orphan boy who roamed the land with his dog. They survived on berries and roots, and sometimes the dog would catch a rabbit. No one would take in the boy as he wandered from camp to camp in search of a home.

One particularly cold night, he came upon a camp. Because the bison hunt had been poor, the people had little food. The families, with more children than they could feed, regretted that none of them could adopt the orphan boy. In the camp was an old man whose children were grown. He took the boy into his tepee and called him Grandson.

The boy was warm and happy in his new home. Even his dog happily carried packs for the people as they followed the bison herds. "Grandfather," the boy said one day, "I am grateful to you and the people. I wish to do something for you."

"Work and hunt with us," the old man replied. "That is the greatest gift."

"But I wish to do more," the boy insisted. "I wish to do the greatest thing your people have ever known."

"Well," the old man said, "there is a legendary place in the mountains said to be home to magnificent beasts larger than elks and stronger than dogs. Perhaps you could find them."

So the boy took his dog into the mountains. After 10 days, the boy was stopped by a great owl. "What do you want here?" the owl demanded.

"I have come in search of the legendary elk dogs," the boy said.

"They are deep in the mountain," the owl said, pointing his wing to the west. "Over there."

The boy continued westward up the mountain, and after 10 more days, he was stopped by a wolverine, who growled, "What do you want here?"

"I seek the legendary elk dogs," the boy replied.

The wolverine snorted, "They are deep in the mountain." He raised his paw and pointed west. "Over there."

After another 10 days, the boy and his dog had eaten all their food, so the dog caught a snowshoe hare. He gave the hare to the boy. "Please do not eat me!" the hare cried. "I heard you were looking for the elk dogs. I can show you where to find them."

The boy released the hare and followed it deep into the mountain, where they saw a herd of elk dogs grazing on spring grass and nibbling yellow flowers. The boy captured the leader and climbed on his back. Clutching the long, black hair on the elk dog's neck, the boy rode the beast down the mountain, and the whole herd thundered behind.

Thanks to the swift elk dog, the boy raced down the mountain in just three days. When the boy brought the herd of elk dogs to the old man, he said proudly, "Here is my gift to you, Grandfather. Now we can follow the bison herds and never go hungry again."

It was true. The Blackfoot Indians became the greatest horse riders and bison hunters in Montana.

GLOSSARY

Aboriginal – of or relating to the Australian Aborigines, the people who inhabited Australia before the arrival of European settlers

auditory – related to hearing

captive-breeding – being bred and raised in a place from which escape is not possible

cultures – particular groups in a society that share behaviors and characteristics that are accepted as normal by that group

domesticated – tamed to be kept as a pet or used as a work animal

ecological – having to do with the interdependence of organisms living together in an environment

evaporates – changes from liquid to invisible vapor, or gas

evolved – gradually developed into a new form

extinct – having no living members

feral – in a wild state after having been domesticated

genetic – relating to genes, the basic physical units of heredity

gestation – the period of time it takes a baby to develop inside its mother's womb

hierarchy – a system in which people, animals, or things are ranked in importance one above another

inbreeding – the breeding of individuals that are related to one another

land bridge – a piece of land connecting two landmasses that allowed people and animals to pass from one place to another

muzzle – the projecting part of an animal's face that includes the nose and mouth

nuisance – something annoying or harmful to people or the land

nutrients – substances that give an animal energy and help it grow

paleontologists – scientists who study extinct animals, plants, and other organisms

SELECTED BIBLIOGRAPHY

Fuller, Alexandra. "Mustangs: Spirit of the Shrinking West." National Geographic Online. http://ngm .nationalgeographic.com/2009/02/wild-horses /fuller-text.

Halls, Kelly Milner. *Wild Horses: Galloping through Time*. Plain City, Ohio: Darby Creek, 2008.

National Mustang Association. "Wild Horses and Burros." http://www.nmautah.org/wild.htm.

Prioli, Carmine. *The Wild Horses of Shackleford Banks*. Winston-Salem, N.C.: John F. Blair, 2007.

Stillman, Deanne. *Mustang: The Saga of the Wild Horse in the American West*. New York: Mariner Books, 2009.

United States Department of the Interior, Bureau of Land Management. "National Wild Horse and Burro Program." http://www.blm.gov/wo/st/en/prog/whbprogram.html.

Note: Every effort has been made to ensure that any websites listed above were active at the time of publication. However, because of the nature of the Internet, it is impossible to guarantee that these sites will remain active indefinitely or that their contents will not be altered.

Routinely slaughtered for pet food and other products, wild horses need human supporters to save them.

INDEX